CLINICAL PSYCHOLOGY REFLECTIONS
VOLUME 1

CONNOR WHITELEY

No part of this book may be reproduced in any form or by any electronic or mechanical means. Including information storage, and retrieval systems, without written permission from the author except for the use of brief quotations in a book review.

This book is NOT legal, professional, medical, financial or any type of official advice.

Any questions about the book, rights licensing, or to contact the author, please email connorwhiteley@connorwhiteley.net

Copyright © 2022 CONNOR WHITELEY

All rights reserved.

DEDICATION

Thank you to all my readers without you I couldn't do what I love.

INTRODUCTION

Clinical Psychology, at least in the United Kingdom, places a massive emphasis on the reflective practitioner. Basically, encouraging people in clinical psychology to be reflective and learn from their experiences.

And I absolutely love clinical psychology and it is truly an amazing area of psychology. Since clinical psychology takes facts and theory and applies them to real life so we can help people.

That is why I love this area.

As a result of this passion, I'm studying a Psychology With Clinical Psychology degree at the University of Kent, and in my second year I had to do a reflective log.

Allowing me to develop my reflective skills for my possible future career, and I really enjoyed reflecting on different topics within and outside clinical psychology.

However, the reason I'm writing this book is because the feedback from my university lecturer was extremely positive and she encouraged me to continue these reflections.

So the idea of a book of clinical psychology reflections got born as well as whilst this is very different from my normal fact based psychology books. All my thoughts and feelings are based on my experience and research into clinical psychology.

This is going to be great fun!

Who Is This Book For?

At first, I had no idea but after writing these reflections, this book is definitely for university psychology students AND professionals.

Students will love this because these reflections will give you great perspectives and topics into areas of clinical psychology that aren't talked about in lectures. (They never were for me!)

Then professionals will greatly enjoy this book too because these reflections can act as great reminders and they can inspire too.

In fact, most of these reflections are rather inspiring for everyone.

Overall, this book of reflections can help you learn more and deepen your understanding of clinical psychology.

Who Am I?

I always love to know who writes the nonfiction I read.

Therefore, in case you're like me, I'm Connor Whiteley. The author over 15 psychology books as of June 2021 including an extremely popular clinical psychology book.

Also, I'm the host of the weekly The Psychology World Podcast available on all major Podcast apps and YouTube. Talking about psychology and psychology news.

Finally, I'm a university psychology student at the University of Kent, England. Doing a psychology degree that has a large focus on clinical psychology.

So BUY NOW and let's start reflecting together!

THE PURPOSE AND MANDATE OF CLINICAL PSYCHOLOGY

This reflection was initially inspired by the integrity reflection later in the book. But as I love this idea so much I needed to bring this forward.

In addition, there is no 'official' mandate of clinical psychology so of course this is my own opinions and thoughts.

Therefore, if you're a clinical psychologist then you know it is our job as clinical psychologists or people interested in clinical psychology to help improve people's lives and to alleviate psychological distress.

Now, I want to turn this into a mandate because this is the entire point of clinical psychology.

Since clinical psychology's entire existence comes back to this purpose. Without this purpose, there is no clinical psychology.

Because everything from the clinical research to the therapist to the clinical paperwork it all comes back to improving people's lives.

If there were no researchers to research cases and treatments for depression, anxiety or any other mental health conditions. Then it would be next to impossible for the practitioner to help improve their client's lives and alleviate their psychological distress.

Yet these researchers are and must be guided by this mandate. Because if their research doesn't help distress or improve lives. Then I am sorry to say it is of no use to clinical psychology.

Not because it is bad research (necessarily) but because it doesn't support the clinical psychology mandate.

Applying this mandate to clinical psychologists and other practitioners, it is vital that they are and must be guided by this mandate. Because everything a clinical psychologist does is in our client's interest. From advocacy to conferring with our team members to the therapy itself.

Everything a clinical psychologist does is to help alleviate their client's psychological distress and improve their lives.

If a clinical psychologist has done the mandate then they're done an amazing job.

It isn't always easy to help alleviate psychological distress or improve lives. But it is amazing when you can.

And if you follow this mandate and use it as an internal compass then hopefully this will help you in clinical psychology.

I never ever say these things to scare you.

I say them to make you realise clinical psychology is an amazing area of psychology to love and want to work in.

So please remember the mandate and read on, there are a lot of amazing things to reflect on…

SHOULD PSYCHOLOGISTS BE ABLE TO PRESCRIBE MEDICATION?

Today on my podcast The Psychology World Podcast, I did an episode on the for and against arguments for should psychologists be able to prescribe medication as treatment.

So, the episode introduced the background information and the for and against arguments.

Personally, I found the background information rather interesting because in 5 states of the USA psychologists can prescribe medication, and I discussed the training required as well.

Therefore, I think it's interesting to think about psychology in these states has developed.

However, this raises a number of valid questions about prescribing privileges.

Why hasn't this spread to other states or countries?

Could it mean it doesn't work?

What other factors could lead to these States to adopt prescribing privileges? Such as: a shortage of psychiatrists or prescribing doctors?

Additionally, I really liked exploring the topic because the BPS have raised this debate in The Psychologist in 2020. And if psychologists don't engage with the topic then others will make the decisions about prescribing rights for psychologists without their input.

Afterwards, I explained the pros and cons of prescribing rights. In my opinion, I can understand why prescribing privileges could be a good idea. As it might increase access to mental health treatment and it could free up doctors, as I said on the podcast.

However, in addition to the other disadvantages, I mentioned in the episode. My central concern still remains. As a profession, we need to move towards Formulation being engrained at every level of a service, and we must focus on the biopsychosocial model. I have discussed this in my Formulation In Psychotherapy book and Lucy Johnstone says the same.

So, my concern is if we allow psychologists to get

prescribing rights, then could this push psychology backwards to the biomedical model?

And we place less of an emphasis on psychological and social factors as we can simply give medication to solve the condition?

Again, it might only be a school of thought within psychology, but surely that's still a lot of psychologists?

Regardless of what happens psychologists need to act in the interest of their clients and not in the interest of ourselves or the service. We are there to improve lives and alleviate psychological distress.

GENETIC TREATMENTS FOR MENTAL CONDITIONS

This week for my biological psychology module seminar, I had to read a paper called: Plomin and College (2001): Beyond Inheritance and I really wanted to reflect on this paper. As it mentioned Clinical psychology in a passing note.

Due to it mentioned that if psychology can find specific genes. Then it's possible to find genetically based treatment options for mental conditions.

Personally, I can understand the logic as it would be amazing, cheaper and much more effective than current biological treatment. If we had a magic bullet where we could give someone a drug that targets specific genes, and the mental conditions goes away.

However, as my podcast audience and readers know, I am a massive opponent to the biomedical model.

And this is what this idea would mean. It would be reductionist and propose that everything is down to 'simple' genetics.

Whilst, completely informing the cognitive and social factors because how would a genetic treatment help a depressed person with a negative cognitive style or someone with a bad parental relationship?

Therefore, in my opinion, I love the simple idea of this tiny paragraph. As it could save people time as you might only need to take this treatment one. It could save services money as this treatment is a magic bullet. As well as it could prevent the service or organisation from confounding the mental condition. Since the client spends virtually no time with the service.

On the other hand, I strongly believe in this is a reductionist way of thinking. That reinforces the biomedical model. And it neglects the social and cognitive factors that are just as important as the genetic factors.

Therefore, I want to wrap p this entry by stressing the importance of the biopsychosocial model. So, we acknowledge the different factors and how they interact.

Also, I want to emphasise the importance of formulation as instead of creating a magic bullet for the type of condition. Where we're label people. We need to acknowledge that they are a person and we need to tailor make a treatment for them and their unique difficulties.

THE IMPORTANCE OF REFLECTION IN CLINICAL PSYCHOLOGY

Whilst I talk about the reflective practitioner in my Clinical Psychology book, I wanted to do a bit more of a personal reflection on why reflecting is important in clinical psychology.

There are two angles I want to perceive this from. And yes, I think after my perception reflection, I will mention it from time to time because it is important.

Firstly, I want to take this reflection from the viewpoint of a psychology student that is passionate about clinical psychology.

Therefore, it's important to reflect on what we've learnt in clinical psychology because it helps us to have a deeper understanding of the topic. And it helps with deep processing from cognitive psychology which helps out memory.

However, the most important reason to reflect is because we are the next generation of clinical psychologists. So, if we reflect on something and we know it needs to change then we can.

We have the power to do that, but without reflecting and knowing something needs to be improved we can't.

Personally, if you've read my [Formulation In Psychotherapy](#) book, the other reflections or listen to The Psychology World Podcast. You know how passionate I am about coming away from the biomedical model and ensuring formulation is used. Yet if I hadn't reflected or learnt about this amazing topic, I wouldn't be able to have this opinion.

Therefore, I really want to encourage psychology students to reflect on what they've learnt not just for their own education but for their own thinking too.

Moving onto the other angle, I want to discuss why it's critical for clinical psychologists to reflect.

The main reason is really simple. It's all about improvement because as a field, clinical psychology must always be improving and hoping to improve.

As a result, clinical psychologists should reflect on the services they work in. Like, is the service confounding the client's difficulties, is the service being as effective as it could, could they decrease the bureaucracy and so on.

All of these questions and more could help the service to improve and become even better at alleviating the psychological distress of the clients.

Equally, the clinical psychologists could reflect on a technique, and whilst this is more aimed towards the clinical psychologists in research. It can still apply to everyone because by reflecting on a technique you might pick up on a flaw or something the technique lacks. Meaning you might want to improve it allowing the field of clinical psychology to develop further.

For example, if you use a self-reported questionnaire to measure depression with your clients. But you feel as if it didn't really explore the interpersonal relations as well as it could. You might want to improve it and a better, more holistic technique is always good.

This, as you can see in this example, it's good to reflect on techniques clinical psychology uses because things can always be improved. And you might be the person to do it!

The final and most important area a clinical psychologist needs to reflect on is themselves. This is critical because reflection allows you to grow and develop as a clinical psychologist. As well as it allows you to learn things that you can use in the future.

For instance, let's say you're a Cognitive Behavioural Therapist and you helped a boy who hated the talking side of Cognitive Behavioural Therapy and wasn't too keen on the more visual aspects of it. But you found the boy loved the storytelling. You might reflect on the case to see what you could have done differently. Like, could you have introduced yourself or the talking better? Could you have done the visual aspects differently?

Then you could reflect on what you're learned so you might want to how you did the storytelling and how this helped changed the automatic thoughts and other CBT concepts.

So you could use it in the future perhaps.

Consequently, whilst that example was completely fictional. I hope you can perceive the importance of self reflection in clinical psychology.

Overall, in this reflection, I've spoken a lot about being reflective in clinical psychology. This I want to finish up by saying reflecting can be great fun and it gives us and the field of clinical psychology a chance to grow and develop.

So please, go out into the world and have fun reflecting. You never know what you might find!

WHY IS CONTINUED PROFESSIONAL DEVELOPMENT IMPORTANT?

To start off I must, must say that CPD Stands for Continued Professional Development, and I need to explain this because for the first year of my clinical psychology degree. People kept saying CPD without ever, ever explaining it.

Which I think is pretty funny because in clinical psychology you just know what CPD is and everyone knows it.

And we do the same thing in the author community. My favourite is when an author says: "I'm thinking of joining IS. thoughts?"

Then newer authors panic.

But us longer term authors just know what IS is. (It's another place we sell our books)

Anyway, the reason why I want to reflect on CPD is because I know a few clinical psychology students think CPD is a pointless waste of time.

But it's probably one of the most important things within clinical psychology,

Because clinical psychology CPD is all about learning and I'll sum up everything here: if a clinical psychologist graduated in the 1950s and didn't learn about new psychotherapies and models. Do you really think they would be helping clients?

And that's the entire point of CPD, making sure we keep learning. We learn about new therapies, new findings and new things that we can take back to our therapy rooms and use with our clients. To improve their lives, and alleviate their psychological distress.

Personally, this is one of the reasons why I love clinical psychology. Because so few other professions make learning such a critical focus.

I love learning and thinking. It's why I do courses, go to university, listen to podcasts and write my books.

Because I want to keep learning and expanding my knowledge base.

But I might have taken this a bit far in 2020 as I read Beekeeping For Dummies. A great book though!

So what I want to say is don't see CPD as some terrible job requirement.

Clinical psychology is amazing I can promise you that.

And you bought this book without being told to (thank you!) so maybe you like learning more than you think.

THE IMPORTANCE OF SELF-CARE IN CLINICAL PSYCHOLOGY

This reflection might be one of the most important in this book, hence why it's near the front. Due to self care and making sure that us as current or future clinical psychologists are okay and protected.

I know within all clinical psychology jobs that I know about, there are structures and procedures in place to protect clinical psychologists. But I still believe strongly that the concept of self-care is vital to reflect on.

As a result in clinical psychology, we are bound to see things that make us uncomfortable, and will harm our own mental health at that moment or over time.

Also, of course, this depends on the sector of clinical psychology you work in.

For example, if you work mainly with teenagers with depression and anxiety. Then hearing some of the tragic stories will upset you and possibly decrease your mental health.

Another slightly more severe are in eating disorders and hearing those stories about their body image and why our clients are making sure they have horrific eating patterns. These can be upsetting.

(Please forgive me if anything in the paragraph above is slightly off. My knowledge of eating disorders is surface level at best)

Then the last example is the extreme where if you work with people (even teenagers or children) who self harm and want to kill themselves.

Just seeing these injuries and learning these stories are so important, but extremely upsetting.

This is why I couldn't work in this area. Well, that and some personal reasons.

As well as this is why I admired the hell out of therapists and clinical psychologists that work in this area.

So after briefly looking at these areas. We need to talk about self care because it is so critical that clinical psychologists are mentally protected from the job.

Due to if our mental health suffers then we can't do our jobs properly, and most importantly we cant help people.

This is why it's great so many clinical psychologists in the UK, at least, have their own therapist or professional they can check in with and see if they're okay.

Also, I think it's extremely helpful here to mention as a current or future clinical psychologist. It's very important to develop strategies to help you cope.

So, you might want to check out the tens of episodes on mental health and strategies on The psychology World Podcast.

Overall, if you ever go into clinical psychology, please help people but look after yourself too.

And remember if your mental health needs help, you can't help others effectively.

But that's okay. Your mental health takes priority.

THOUGHTS ON PSYCHOLOGY OF RELIGION

This week I finished reading a new book on the psychology of religion.

Now, originally I wasn't going to do a reflection because I tend to religion and politics are best to avoid unless you the person.

Although, I will do a brief reflection.

Therefore, the book mentioned a lot of interesting things. Like, children aren't inheritably more likely to believe in God. This is supported by Paiget's theory as the god concept is rather abstract, and children don't tend to form abstract thought until age 11.

Also, it mentioned that religion doesn't naturally make you moral. There are other factors as well as it expanded upon topics of religious socialisation and the restrictive morals of religion.

Anyway, linking this book to clinical practice, I want to stress that when we're in clinical settings and in therapy sessions. We must respect [people belief's and we must not be prejudice or discriminate against them.

It is their right to believe.

Therefore, in clinical settings, we must culturally adapt our sessions and be mindful of our reflectivity. To try and ensure the client benefits as much as possible from the therapy.

Consequently, if we need to change how the therapy is done slightly to make it more approachable or how the setting to make the client more comfortable then we should, or at least, consider it.

At the end of the day, it is our job as clinical psychologists to help the client live a better happier life and their religion will impact this in one way or another.

Reference

The Psychology of Religion by Vassilis Sargoglou.

COMMENTS ON PSYCHOLOGY TV PROGRAMMES

Usually, I'm not much of a 'psychology' TV programmes because 99% of them tend to get psychology completely wrong.

However, I've recently discovered a new 'drama' I guess you could call it that, and it was very good. It was called Evil.

In short, it's a clinical psychologist who is hired by the catholic church to assess 'miracles' and other supposed holy things. Like, demonic possession.

Also, I like it because it has pretty dark scenes.

Nevertheless, the reason why I'm talking about it in a reflective journal is because this fictional programme clearly shows how mental conditions can manifest, as well as lead people to believe they're demonically possessed. Where they could be psychotic or suffer from schizophrenia.

Overall, this highlights the need with clinical psychology to be respectful of people's beliefs and we need to acknowledge that mental conditions can manifest in different ways.

Finally, I like that this program shows briefly the pressure that some legal professionals put on clinical psychologists as expert witnesses to sat the 'right' thing. I know this is rare but it reminds us that we never 'bow down' to that pressure. Or we risk the integrity of the profession, let alone ourselves.

EPISODE 61 OF THE PSYCHOLOGY WORLD PODCAST REFLECTION

Yesterday, I recorded and interviewed New York Times and USA Today Best-selling author J. F Penn and we talked about Carl Jung, the psychology of religion and much more.

However, the reason why the interview has made its way into this reflective log is because this gave me a chance to improve my interview skills as I haven't interview someone for ages.

This is always useful since as a clinical psychologist I would be interviewing clients about their difficulties.

Whilst, I was very organised and the interview went great. I must confess I did stutter a lot in some sections.

Now, I've never seen this as a problem per sat but

this is a skill I need to work out in the future for my hopeful clinical psychology career.

In addition, I wanted to reflect on a particular part of the interview where Joanna and I were discussing Carl Jung and his ideas about alchemy. This I loved because he believed in short, that people were base metals and could grow and develop into beautiful things.

This idea I love because it is a great way to think about people, and as clinical psychologists, it is our job to not only help people further their own personal difficulties. But to help them to live more fulfilled lives.

Yet it is our job to help them to realise their full potential so they can turn from base metals into something beautiful and precious. Without making this sound like a self-improvement thing!

POSITIVES OF VIDEO GAMES

As a quick entry into this reflective log, I wanted to talk about a new study, I quickly spoke about the psychology news section of The Psychology World Podcast.

I read about a new study that found playing video games for longer can increase well-being.

Now, I'll fully admit the effect of this was small. But an effect is still an effect and the methodology was very good.

Therefore, I wanted to discuss the findings in relation to clinical psychology.

Whether it be at an individual, interpersonal or family level. Video games can conflict for several reasons. Yet one of these ideas is the parents quite rightfully being concerned about their child's wellbeing in relation to gaming.

Now, I'm going to keep this quite general, and I'll ignore other factors here. However, if this reason is a source of conflict within the family and contributes to difficulties and other outcomes as outlined in systemic therapy. This, as clinical psychologists or who those wanting to become, we have to inform the parents about the growing amount of research supporting playing video games and wellbeing.

Also, there can be a social aspect to online. This is especially relevant during the second UK lockdown.

Of course, all research has limitations and I'm not saying we should encourage people to play video games for long periods of time. Since people still need real human contact, exercise, going outside, etc.

However, I believe this piece of research and other studies like it, should have an awareness in clinical psychology. Since video games can be a source of conflict within families.

DIVERSITY WITHIN CLINICAL PSYCHOLOGY

For a change, I wanted to talk about diversity in the field of clinical psychology, because I truly believe it's great there's at least one professional where women are in highly paid positions.

However, the problem with the field o clinical psychology is the vast majority are white middle-class women.

Although, the one benefit of this, if we go by stereotypes, is women tend to more open to difficulties and talking about them compared to men in my opinion.

Yet this is still very problematic because every class tends to have a certain experience and it is this commonality that makes people 'click' and this helps the therapeutic alliance.

Therefore, if I needed therapy then I would find this difficult with a white middle-class woman to some extent. As yes, I am middle class and white but I am male.

So, I would have been exposed to different societal pressures, expectations and experiences.

Therefore, I might be more open to talking to a male but I'm not sure. But I know other men would prefer to talk to men.

I would elaborate but I have some more personal thoughts on this topic.

Additionally, black people would probably be more comfortable talking to a fellow black person. Since they can discuss their own black experiences.

And the same goes for members of the LGBT+ community.

Overall, it is imperative that we increase diversity within clinical psychology so we can help clients get the best therapist for them and they can have a very good therapeutic relationship and this increases the likelihood of having successful therapy and living better lives.

CLINICAL PSYCHOLOGY IN HEALTH SETTINGS

So, I've just watched the first 30 minutes of an episode of My 600LB Life. I don't normally watch it but this makes its way into this clinical log because this female on the program had a medication condition that was caused and maintained by her obesity.

Now, this is a prime example of the biopsychosocial model. Due to the female could have a medical operation to fix her medical condition. Yet this is useless as unless her mental processes are changed to become healthier then she will get obese once more, and her medical condition will return.

Therefore, this highlights the immense importance of coming away from the biomedical model and towards the biopsychological model and formulation.

As demonstrated in this case, the psychological causes of obesity must be treated as important as the physical factors. Or the physical factors will only be maintained and never end or be rerated.

THE CLIENT ISN'T POWERLESS AGAINST YOU

As I'm about to write this I almost have to laugh at myself because of how I got the idea for this reflection. As I was watching another episode of My 600LB life with my mum the other day. And I promise you I do not watch that sort of TV regularly.

Anyway, in this episode, the medical doctor had ordered the 600LB woman to go to psychotherapy. Personally, I love how psychotherapy Is used as an umbrella term. But as we all know there a LOT of different types. Over 500 in fact.

Then when she was in psychotherapy she went in and wow… the Tv magic that went on was amazing. But the real purpose of the reflection is in the therapy session the client (the 600LB woman) kept saying yes to everything.

Now I know there was a lot of TV magic going on because the session lasted for 5 minutes apparently and so much was covered. But one of my main issues with how the therapy was portrayed was the client seemed powerless against the therapist.

This is a problem and whilst I know, I know this was only TV but I feel like it's important to take note of this, and stress it.

So there will always, always be a power difference in therapy. That's sadly normal. Yet it is the job of us want-to-be professional therapists to lessen this power difference. By developing a relationship with our clients and helping them to open up and become empowered.

I guess empowerment is another goal in therapy as well.

And the reason why empowerment as well as lessening the power difference in therapy is so critical is because if the client doesn't feel powerful enough to correct or even challenge us. Then the responses we will get from our clients will be biased and aimed to please us.

This helps nobody.

Especially, if our interventions, assessments, formulations, etc. are 'wrong' or skewed due to these answers.

Therefore, please stress without our clients that it's okay to question you. no one is perfect and as I always say therapists bring the expertise in psychology and mental health. But it is the client that brings the expertise in themselves.

So, go on- encourage them to use it!

SOCIAL IDENTITY THEORY IN THERAPY

I absolutely fully admit, this is one of my weirder ideas for my reflections. Since I was revising recently for my social psychology of group exams and I was revising Social identity theory. Then some how I managed to link it to clinical psychology so I thought it would be an interesting theory to reflect on.

Before we reflect on the theory itself, I wanted to briefly recap it in case you need it. Therefore social identity theory (Tajfel & Turner 1981), in essence, proposed that people have ingroups, the groups they belong to, and people are more competitive or don't like outgroups as much as ingroups.

Whilst I know there is more to it than that. That's all the information, we need for this reflection.

However, if you want to read more about social

identity theory, please read Social Psychology for more information.

Moving onto the reflection itself, I think social identity theory does have implications in clinical psychology for two main reasons.

First, it shows the theory behind why clinical psychologists need to develop rapport, therapeutic relations/ alliance and basically help the client to know, like and trust us.

Due to it is only when the client can consider the clinical psychologist or the therapist as part of the ingroup, can the therapy start having an effect.

As we listen to our ingroups members, respect and want to work WITH them.

The last thing a clinical psychologist wants is to have a client who sees them as an enemy outgroup member.

That really won't help the therapy!

Leading me onto my second point, Social Identity Theory also shows why the type of therapist matters.

For example, let's use say the client is a young white British male from a poor area in the north of England without any qualifications higher than a GCSE. (These are the grades you get at 16 years old in the

UK)

Then the therapist is a white woman in her late 50s from a rich part of London in the South of England with her doctorate and she has lived in privilege all her life.

In all honesty, I don't believe my example is too extreme from the types of people in the real world.

As you can see, the therapist is clearly an outgroup member and even if the therapist had extremely good communication and therapist skills. I still strongly believe there would always be this gap or lack of shared experience between them.

Yet I know of cases from my clinical psychology lecturer of were unlikely pairings have just 'clicked' and worked great.

However, what I'm trying to imply is this is why trying to match the client with the right therapist is important. So, the client can feel like they're talking to an ingroup member that understands them and their life.

And this links to other topics like the need for diversity within clinical psychology.

Whilst I had no idea where I was going with this idea at first I truly hope this was an interesting and thought provoking idea for you.

How do you think social identity theory could impact clinical psychology?

PRECEPTION

Wow, this really is one of those topics that are so massive I don't know where to start. And I know I will miss things out but the point of these reflections is to get me and you thinking about these issues in clinical psychology.

Therefore, I originally got the idea for this reflection from my clinical psychology lecturer because she would always put up these Figure Images at the end of the lecture. You know the images where if you look at it one way it's one thing. But if you look at it again it's another thing. They're called Ambiguous Figure Images.

Anyway, she always said the reason she put those up is because clinical psychology is about perception.

Now, there are hundreds of directions I can take this in but I'm going to take the integrative direction here.

And I might bring this back up again in the problem Reflection later on.

In clinical psychology, it is the job of the clinical psychologist to have a great perception of what's going on. Because as I've mentioned before in these reflections and my books, no condition is ever caused by one thing. And this is where I believe perception comes in.

Since a clinical psychologist needs to be able to take a step back, ideally even outside their own therapeutic model, to see the bigger picture and the see what's causing the mental health difficulty from different angles.

For example, if a clinical psychologist had a client with extreme social anxiety and the clinical psychologist was trained in Cognitive Behavioural Therapy. Then this would give them great perception and a great ability to perceive the cognitive causes of the condition.

Yet as I've mentioned before being holistic and looking at the difficulty from all angles is so important.

Due to if the clinical psychologist only looks at the social anxiety through a cognitive lens. Then they might be missing crucial causes or maintaining factors that could have been perceived if they looked at the client's school life, home life or at another level like societal or interpersonal level.

As a result, what I'm trying to say is, whether you are or you're training to be a clinical psychologist or you're just interested in clinical psychology. Please don't limit your perception to what you're narrowly trained in.

Take a step back, open your eyes, ask a peer and always question is there more to this condition than I can perceive?

Sometimes there won't be.

But you never know how this simple question can improve the therapeutic success for your client.

And you never know, you might learn something too!

IS IT REALLY A PROBLEM?

This is a great topic to reflect on within clinical psychology because people typically come to clinical psychologists when they have a 'problem' or other people pick up on a 'problem' and get them to seek professional help.

Now, the reason I think this is important to reflect on is clinical psychologists need to question is something actually a problem or are other people interpreting it as a problem when it isn't?

So, I'll give you a personal example then I'll define a so-called problem in clinical psychology before talking more generally.

To use an extremely personal example, a few years ago because I'm autistic, I like small social groups and I had a best friend who I didn't like their other friends. So, I would like to spend time alone with them because this meant we could talk, have fun and be great friends. Without me having to deal with his friends. Plus, when we at a particular social activity together he had his friends, I had mine.

I know this sounds extremely complex but it worked and we were great best friends.

However because I wanted to spent time with him alone, also because together we were being bullied by other people started to think there was a problem.

Long story short, a lot of things happened causing me extreme psychological distress all because of a problem that only existed in the minds of others.

I know that was quick and not the full story but I think you can understand it. Me and my friend had a way of working. Other people didn't understand, or bother trying to, they thought it was a problem causing a lot of distress.

And this misidentification of a 'problem' is not uncommon and sometimes clinical psychologists can miss this because of the sick role bias. This is where a clinical psychologist looks for something wrong with the client because they have come to the psychologist.

Leading on from this, in clinical psychology a 'problem' or, as clinical psychologists prefer, mental health difficulty is a maladaptive behaviour to cope with life, for lack of a better term.

Therefore, if you only a look at my example then use me and my friend found a way to cope with both our autism, friendship and bullying. But was it maladaptive?

No.

Meaning it was not a problem.

Yet depression, anxiety and self-harming, these are mental health difficulties because these are maladaptive ways of dealing with the world.

Overall, what I'm trying to say is in clinical psychology, you need to be aware when a client comes to you and talks about their difficulties and you should question are these actually maladaptive or have people told you they are.

And this reminds me of two things.

I once watched a TED talk with a schizophrenic woman and she only started to experience 'problems' when people told her she wasn't normal. And hearing voices is weird. Hence showing how other people's beliefs can create problems.

But the most important aspect of this reflection to think about is clinical psychology is all about alleviating psychological distress and improving people's lives.

So, if there are problems or mental health difficulties in our client's life then that is what clinical psychologists are for.

If there aren't difficulties then it's our job to help the people to realise they're fine.

My final message in this reflection is to relax and ask the question: is this really a problem?

Most of the time they'll be a clear mental health difficulty.

But otherwise, you might need to take a step back and ask the question.

THE IMPORTANCE OF SOCIETAL FACTORS

In my Formulation In Psychotherapy book, I wrote a chapter on the social constructivist viewpoint, and I want to take a step back away from formulation and reflect more generally about it.

Therefore, the social constructivist viewpoint looks at how our culture and society influence our behaviour.

Now, I know this impacts everyone to varying degrees. For example, one reason it affects men is because men are supposed to be stronger, emotionless and not show weakness,

Yet as I discussed in Cognitive Psychology and on the Psychology World Podcast this is rubbish. And all these stereotypes are wrong and men should be able to express emotion.

In addition, it affects women because some aspects of society teach us that women are less intelligent, emotional wrecks and less competent. This leads to all sorts of inequalities and negative mental health outcomes.

Also, in some places, women are meant to get married early and be a baby factory.

Of course, all of these are wrong and disgraceful. Women are intelligent and have the right to choose how they live.

However, the real point of this reflection is to look at members of the LGBT+ and the black communities. Since these people as do other groups, experience more unique and specialised difficulties.

For example, black people, yet I can't speak too much about it because I'm white, experience difficulties from racism, outright discrimination, implicit racism but also stereotype threat that brings on psychological distress. All these pressures and difficulties can cause a black person's mental health to decrease.

Then the last group I want to discuss before linking this to clinical psychology is gay people. Due to these people suffer difficulties from growing up in a world that doesn't necessarily accept them. and this is a difficult reflection to write because everyone is unique and has their own experience.

Although, one perspective for a gay person would be struggling with who they are because they live in a social world and family that is homophobic. Leading the person to believe they will lose the family they love because their family will not agree with them.

Then you have the wider issues about discrimination, bullying amongst others.

Overall, all these different society-level factors can cause or play a role in different mental health conditions and put pressure and psychological distress on a person.

As a result in clinical psychology, this links back to perception, it's important whenever you have a client to consider how the society they live in affects them.

And this is especially important when you're dealing or helping a client from a marginalised group.

Since if we take the example of a self-harming gay person then whilst you could help them at the cognitive and interpersonal level. The real key might be helping them to understand it's okay to be gay. As well as helping them to find better coping mechanisms when they encounter abuse.

On the whole, the entire point of this reflection is to always consider the role society has on the mental health difficulties and conditions.

Sometimes it won't play a major role.

But other times it might be the critical precipitating or maintaining factor and that is where our focus must be.

STRESSING CONFIDENTIALITY

When I wrote my clinical psychology book, I originally kept the confidentiality section to maybe 300 or less words. But now I wish that I hadn't because I now really want to expand this section to discuss why confidentiality in clinical psychology is so important and as that book isn't due an update for another year or 2 I wanted to talk about confidentiality here.

Due to in clinical psychology and psychotherapy, we are basically asking people to trust us and tell us some extremely uncomfortable things about themselves. I like to imagine or compare this to telling your grandma about your nighttime life. You simply wouldn't want to do it or you would find it extremely uncomfortable. And that is what we are doing in clinical psychology.

Now, I am not criticising clinical psychology because

we need to know these things in order to fulfil our purpose and help to alleviate their psychological distress.

However, if we continue to think about these uncomfortable truths. Just imagine if that person had difficulties that their parents or caregivers didn't know about. Like, suicidal thoughts or attempts or self-harm.

This is where we get into more difficult territory because these are even more difficult to tell someone about. As well as this also stresses the need for good rapport, therapeutic alliance amongst other topics.

Yet the purpose of this reflection is to talk about confidentiality. And this is where we need to put ourselves in our client's shoes. Because they do not know who we report to, nor do they know how much is shared between therapists and they really don't know how or if we share information with parents or other loved ones.

Possibly leading them not to share critical things with us over fears of information sharing.

In addition, I should add that we don't know what their home life is like. You never ever know if the person knows they have a condition but they've taken a risk by coming to see you. Due to their parents or their community don't respect therapy or think they have a condition.

Therefore, to wrap up this reflection, I need to say please clinical psychologists, people interested in clinical psychology and everyone else. In a therapy session stress, what confidentiality is, what it covers and most importantly the limits of confidentially. By simply taking to a few minutes to talk about confidentiality, you might be able to increase sharing and most importantly increase the chance of therapeutic success. That is all we want in clinical psychology.

PSYCHOLOGY, CLIMATE CHANGE AND THE IMPORTANCE OF PSYCHOLOGY

I know this isn't strictly related to clinical psychology but this is still a reflection, and I'll probably find a way how to apply this to clinical psychology. So it's going in here.

I decided to write this reflection because of an article I saw in The Psychologist June 2021 edition from the British Psychological Society. And I read the first line or two saying how psychology is vital in fighting against climate change because climate change is caused by human behaviour. Which of course psychologists are experts in.

Additionally, I've just written up a section of my personality psychology book on how Right Wing Authoritarianism causes climate change denial.

Therefore, I wanted to reflect on the importance of psychology. Because I strongly believe since psychology covers all of human behaviour. It means it covers everything. from the obvious like memory, thinking, and social groups to the less obvious personality, climate change and sexuality.

Personally, I know this is great because I LOVE psychology. Due to there is so much to explore and there is always, always something more to learn.

Equally, this is what makes psychology a pain at times. As a result of it's so broad, sometimes we either get lost in everything or we forget that psychology can be applied to it.

Consequently, I'm happy psychology is looking at climate change. We need to understand why some people are climate change deniers and are happy to let the earth be damaged and let humanity suffer both now and in the long run. This must change.

But let's think boarder too and apply psychology to other problems.

Linking this to clinical psychology, I'm surprised I managed to find a link. I really do encourage you with this reflection to think about how clinical psychology could be missing something, it's very possible that we've missed something and not applied psychology (at least not fully in the mainstream) to something that affects mental health, psychological distress and therapy.

As well as I want to finish up this reflection by encouraging you and saying if there is something you want to explore within clinical psychology that hadn't been fully applied yet. Then do it!

Go!

Have fun and explore this great new area. You never know if this might advance the field of clinical psychology or what impacts you possibly might have in the future.

REFLECTIONS OF EPISODE 95

Yesterday, I released episode 95 of the psychology world podcast (available on all major podcast apps and YouTube) and it was on what parents should know about screen time?

(And there are a few clinical psychology points in the episode)

Now, I'm not going to reflect on the actual content per say but there are boarder nuggets of information that I wanted to reflect on. Yet it is a great episode so I highly recommend that you listen to it or read the transcript as connorwhiteley.net/podcast

Therefore, the first thing I want to reflect on is I mentioned that sometimes when children are dealing with a mental health difficulty. They can use technology to hide from the causes of the difficulties.

Now, this I think is well worth a mention because again clinical psychology is all about taking a step back and seeing the bigger picture. Due to 99% of all parents would say the technology is causing the mental health difficulty and that's the end of the so-called problem.

And as that's the natural way to think, we as clinical psychologists or people interested in clinical psychology might get caught in that trap.

We cannot allow this.

Consequently, it's so important in clinical psychology to take a step back and actually question: are the parents right? Is it the screen media?

Also this would be a great time to actually talk to the child because I found to some extent the parents haven't spoken to the child to see if the screen media was the cause or not.

Or the child might not have felt comfortable enough to tell what's going on with their parents. This is whether clinical psychologists come in.

Overall, the endpoint of this first thing is always remember to take a step back, see the bigger picture and remember the importance of perception.

Following on from this, the final thing I want to

reflect on is the importance of strong relationships as protective factors against mental health difficulties.

Since in the podcast episode, I spoke about how having a good relationship between the caregiver and the child is critical for so many reasons.

And this links into clinical psychology perfectly because it shows the importance of intervening at the interpersonal level and looking at the family level. There is so much to this for this reflection. Yet in general, this is important to look at as part of the bigger picture.

Due to until you look you have no idea how the family is impacting the mental health condition or difficulty.

Since the family could be maintaining the difficulty and condition, they could be causing it or they might not be interested

An example of the above would be if the parents only show interest in the child now they're depressed, what would be the motivation for the child to change?

Another example is the parents could be causing the difficulty by their behaviour, bullying or attitudes towards the child.

Also, the worse thing that could happen is the therapy

could fail simply because the person doesn't have the support back home to change and improve their lives.

Overall, I want to wrap up by saying in clinical psychology, it is so important to try and look at everything. I know it always isn't possible but it's important to try. The success of the therapy might depend or not, on how the family influences the mental health difficulty.

Of course, the family won't always matter, but maybe, just maybe it's the key to helping out your client.

THE PSYCHDELYIC FINDING AND INTEGRITY

Ive been meaning to do this for a while but I really wanted to reflect on a topic I covered in the psychology news section in episode 95 of The Psychology World Podcast.

Therefore, the news article basically mentioned that researchers that admitted to using psychedelics were seen as less creditable compared to non-users.

This I think is rather interesting because I'll admit that I haven't seen or done research into psychedelics. Yet I have some limited awareness of their benefits on conditions like depression.

Anyway, what I think is interesting is that people could question the creditability of the researchers due to the researchers being possibly seen as immoral, biased or even criminal. But this all comes back to integrity. And this is what this reflection is all about.

Since integrity is so important in clinical psychology for two main reasons.

The first is in clinical psychology research, it is critical for the researcher to have integrity. So, the results can be trusted and if they're significant (I'm not talking about statistically significant) the research can be adopted by wider clinical psychology, and be used to improve the lives of our clients.

However without integrity then the research is unlikely to be trusted and even if the results are amazing and could transform areas of clinical psychology. It is extremely unlikely for this research to be adopted as the field of clinical psychology just can't take that risk because of the lack of integrity.

The second reason is in clinical practice, integrity is critical for so many reasons. For example, if you're known as having low integrity then your clients will have a hard time trusting or believing in you. Possibly leading them to hold things back, not do the homework and do other behaviours that will greatly harm therapeutic success.

Overall, most certainly leading this clinical psychologist without integrity to fail in clinical psychology's main goal to improve people's lives and alleviate psychological distress.

Without integrity, this main goal and our purpose is impossible to achieve.

So please if you take anything away from this reflection just remember if you're a clinical psychology student, a professional or anyone in between always keep your integrity. I'm sure you will. But if you're ever faced with a decision that could affect your integrity and creditability. Think.

Is it really worth it?

You never know if your choice could affect the lives of your clients.

THE IMPORTANCE OF POSITIVE SELF-IMAGE

Having a Positive Self Image is so, so critical to our wellbeing. Because it's linked to our self-esteem and a few other mental health concepts. But in this reflection, I want to talk about Positive Self Image from a slightly different viewpoint.

Yet first to give you a little more background information, having a Positive Self Image is so common because there are hundreds of ways that we do this. From engaging in downward social comparison to convincing ourselves the theft was justified.

There are a lot of techniques we use to maintain our self-image as explained in Social Psychology and the Forensic Psychology of Theft, Burglary and Property Crime. And we need this to maintain our wellbeing and self-esteem.

However, if you take this idea and put a clinical psychology lens on it. Then maintaining our client's positive self-image might be a powerful tool. And please note I am NOT drawing on any official research here. I'm just reflecting on this potential idea. But later in the reflection, I will outline how clinical psychology already focuses on this and why it's important.

In addition, in a therapy session, we could explicitly try and help our clients to maintain their self-image as this is related to their wellbeing, and increasing their mental health.

So by improving their self-image so they feel positive and good about themselves. We're improving their mental health too.

Also, this is basically what clinical psychology does anyway.

For example, Cognitive Behaviour Therapy is about helping the person to change their thinking patterns to become more positive. Allowing them to see the world, self and future more positively.

Furthermore, systemic therapy does this to some extent because it helps the difficulties in the family system to change and find better, less maladaptive coping mechanisms.

Linking this to positive self-image, systemic therapy helps the family system improve. allowing the difficulties to decrease and this should lead to the individuals in the system to feel better and have a more positive self-image.

As a result, clinical psychology already makes great use of maintaining a positive self-image and the reason why I wanted to mention this is because we all need to have a positive self-image. Otherwise, our self-esteem and mental health does suffer and we don't want this.

Also, just a thought if you as a professional or in the future as someone interested in clinical psychology, are ever stuck on trying to help your client. Then maybe go back to this very basic idea of a positive self-image.

Maybe just start with your client's positive self-image and over time this might help you to discover other difficulties that need to be addressed.

This is probably one of my most theoretical reflections, but I enjoyed it.

What do you think?

POSTNATAL DEPRESSION

As always 99% of Fridays I record my psychology podcast (and I can't believe I'm actually on episode 97!) and I read a news article that covered the increase in postnatal depression. Therefore, I wanted to reflect on this in a bit more depth.

Firstly, I want to provide a bit of background information and I needed to say how terrible this is, but thankfully clinical psychology can help.

Also, I mentioned on the podcast and of course this isn't official advice but if you or anyone you know is having psychological difficulties with postnatal depression. Please, please, please seek professional help.

Moreover, going onto the background information the article was basically saying that the European postnatal depression rate doubled during the first lockdown.

And whilst it didn't go into the causes in the section I read, I want to reflect on them now.

Since the main cause, but not the only one, of course, has been the lack of a social support network for new mothers. Due to before COVID a new mother and father could go to see and interact with their parents, relatives and friends. Allowing them to talk to them about their struggles and to exchange ideas.

But it also allowed these people to show the new parents what to do and this only goes so far on a laptop or phone screen.

Resulting in the new parents feeling alone and isolated whilst they are dealing with their amazing, wonderful yet stressful baby.

Because having a child is wonderful (if that's what you want) but it is stressful due to the crying, pressures, sleepless nights and more.

Consequently, if we try to link this to clinical psychology. This really shows the importance of making sure we and our clients have a good as well as an effective social support network.

Otherwise, our clients and ourselves will suffer a decrease in their mental health.

So, if you take anything away from this reflection. Please let it be that it is vital to make sure we and our clients have social support networks.

Especially, as we know this is a great protective factor against mental health difficulties.

THE DANGERS OF LANGUAGE

Please know that when I write this reflection I am not talking as a fiction author or anything to do as an author. But your words are powerful.

Especially in clinical psychology

As a future or current professional, our words have the power to hurt and alleviate psychological distress.

Yet they also have the power to hurt our clients, precipitate their difficulties and impede their recovery.

I am NOT trying to scare you but I want to explain why clinical psychology has moved towards certain language instead of the older, more hurtful terms.

This is what I'm going to explain in this reflection.

Problematic words and their solutions

Problems- this is a great example of a bad word to use because you are basically implying to your client that it is their fault. They have a mental health condition and they need to fix it.

The reason for this is because if I said I have money problems. Then you would say this is my fault and I need to fix this.

Whenever someone says they have a problem we think something along the lines of

"Really? Can't you fix it by yourself?"

And as clinical psychology knows as does the diathesis stress model and the biopsychosocial model. A mental health condition is NOT the fault of the client.

So let's stop implying it is, even by accident.

This is why the more neutral term difficulty is better.

"Patient" and "Mental illness/ disorder"

Now both of these words work together and they aren't the best words to use because illness implies the person is suffering from a virus or bacterial infection that can be cured, and it will be fine entirely.

Yet we know that mental health conditions never truly go away. For example, someone with depression can be treated and go into remission.

But the depression's genetic and (to some extent) environmental factors will still be there. The person though will have better coping mechanisms for these factors.

So part of the problem with illness is it gives false hope and it takes away from living with the condition to being magically cured.

However, the main problem with the terms patient and illness is it makes a person sound as if something is wrong with them.

Whilst this is the traditional viewpoint, the modern viewpoint is trying to get people to accept themselves. As well as don't see these mental health conditions as illnesses and themselves as patients.

Instead, clinical psychology is trying to get people (amongst other things) to see these conditions as maladaptive mechanisms that are a part of them. in order to help them deal with everyday life. And there is nothing wrong with trying to cope with life.

Therefore, the terms client and condition are much better as well as less blaming to use.

Overall, the point of this reflection has been about awareness. Because we need to get people aware of the damage these old labels can do. And start getting ourselves and others to use new labels.

So we can blame people less and focus on helping them without our language possibly adding to their difficulties.

Of course, at some point, we will all say something bad by accident. But implying our clients are to blame is simply not an option.

Blame being the keyword there.

SCAFFOLDING

Before anyone even thinks it, I want to reassure people I'm not trying to make a connection between clinical psychology and building scaffolding.

What I am trying to reflect on is my thoughts on the importance of Scaffolding. Since I believe it is absolutely critical as well as I'm sure someone a lot smarter than me could connect scaffolding to formulation.

Anyway for anyone who doesn't know what scaffolding is it's when you provide enough structured support for someone to do it themselves.

Its very common in developmental psychology but clinical psychology uses it too.

And the reason I want to talk about this is because of an off the cuff comment someone I know made. And

I want to expand upon it.

Therefore, we have a family friend and their son is moderately autistic. You wouldn't know it at first but after a while you might suspect it.

But due to their parents constantly telling him. He isn't able to do anything because he's autistic. He basically cannot do anything as an adult.

Now before anyone moans at me I knew this person from their childhood and they were great, and they could do things. They could play, make a great reasonable clever conversation and make a sandwich.

Also, I have met an autistic person who cannot talk, walk or do anything. He was the brother of my childhood best friend.

Therefore, I want to reflect on;

1) Just because a person has a level of autism, or any other type of mental health condition it doesn't mean they are incapable.

It reminds me of the Mental Capacity Act section I did in my clinical psychology book. It mentions don't assume someone is incapable until proven otherwise.

2) Give people as much support as they need to get something done independently. Also known as Scaffolding

Because I truly believe if these family friends helped their child more constructively. Then this child would be able to do more.

Of course, I am not expecting this person to be able to do everything. But with the right support, I truly believe they could have some level of independence.

Overall, I know this is a difficult reflection because I purposefully kept this extremely broad. But hopefully, my points are still clear and very important.

Just something to bear in mind.

What do you think?

Are people with mental health conditions capable of doing things?

MENTAL HEALTH AND LGBT+

As June is Pride month, I thought I would do a Pride reflection and I just want to say upfront I'll be using the term gay because I know these people the best. But the general concept should apply to the rest of the LGBT+ community.

Sorry in advance if I cause offence to someone in this reflection.

Anyway, as a future or current clinical psychologist you will probably come across a gay person at some point and like all minority groups, especially historically (and present) oppressed groups, there will be unique factors that affect their mental health in addition to all the other mental health factors that non-gay people have.

For example, for most gay people the idea of 'coming out' is scary and can even be dangerous. As the person could have the (extreme) stress of them losing their social network, their friends and family. Maybe they might be kicked out and made homeless. Maybe they might be beaten or more horrifically maybe they'll be beaten or something to exercise the gay demon out of them. Leading to trauma.

All of these very possible and very real outcomes play on a gay person's mental health. Leading to all sorts of other difficulties and mental health conditions.

Sadly including self-harm and suicide.

Another example of a unique difficulty that I've heard of is: whilst it's a positive that most gay people can hide their 'abnormality' unlike other discriminated groups. (Like black people) Sometimes gay people feel like they're lost or don't know who they are. Because they're:

1) having to lie to everyone to say they like to opposite sex when they really don't.

Or 2) they're suppressing this part of themselves because the society has taught them being gay is horrific and mentally wrong, and gays must die and so on.

(Okay this last one isn't explicit, but I do feel like that sometimes)

So all of this leads to difficulties and challenges for their mental health. All because society has told them they are wrong.

Then the last unique factor I can think of off the top of my head is finding a safe space to express themselves and talk about their difficulties and maintain their mental health.

Because please forgive my oversimplification but black people tend to live in a community, (like certain areas of London) and women can be friends rather easily with other women. Therefore, making these two groups find people that have experienced similar difficulties.

However, for some gay people, this is extremely difficult. Especially, if you live in a neighbourhood without many gay social spots (couldn't think of a better word) and in a loving family that doesn't accept gays overly well.

Meaning these gay people are left alone without anyone to talk to.

Again all these factors play into their mental health over time.

So is there a point to this reflection?

No.

Not really- just please bear in mind that gay people are literally just that- people.

Personally, I don't really understand why being gay is made such a big thing of from both sides.

To me, gay people are just people who like their own sex.

So when it comes to clinical psychology maybe treat them like any other client but make sure you listen to them if these unique or common difficulties come up,

If nothing else, they're interesting to hear about and of course never ever discriminate against anyone.

https://www.subscribepage.com/psychologyboxset

Thank you for reading.

I hoped you enjoyed it.

If you want a FREE book and keep up to date about new books and project. Then please sign up for my newsletter at www.connorwhiteley.net/

Have a great day.

CHECK OUT THE PSYCHOLOGY WORLD PODCAST FOR MORE PSYCHOLOGY INFORMATION!

AVAILABLE ON ALL MAJOR PODCAST APPS.

About the author:

Connor Whiteley is the author of over 30 books in the sci-fi fantasy, nonfiction psychology and books for writer's genre and he is a Human Branding Speaker and Consultant.

He is a passionate warhammer 40,000 reader, psychology student and author.

Who narrates his own audiobooks and he hosts The Psychology World Podcast.

All whilst studying Psychology at the University of Kent, England.

Also, he was a former Explorer Scout where he gave a speech to the Maltese President in August 2018 and he attended Prince Charles' 70th Birthday Party at Buckingham Palace in May 2018.

Plus, he is a self-confessed coffee lover!

All books in 'An Introductory Series':

BIOLOGICAL PSYCHOLOGY 3RD EDITION

COGNITIVE PSYCHOLOGY THIRD EDITION

SOCIAL PSYCHOLOGY- 3RD EDITION

ABNORMAL PSYCHOLOGY 3RD EDITION

PSYCHOLOGY OF RELATIONSHIPS- 3RD EDITION

DEVELOPMENTAL PSYCHOLOGY 3RD EDITION

HEALTH PSYCHOLOGY

RESEARCH IN PSYCHOLOGY

A GUIDE TO MENTAL HEALTH AND TREATMENT AROUND THE WORLD- A GLOBAL LOOK AT DEPRESSION

FORENSIC PSYCHOLOGY

THE FORENSIC PSYCHOLOGY OF THEFT, BURGLARY AND OTHER RIMES AGAINST PROPERTY

CRIMINAL PROFILING: A FORENSIC PSYCHOLOGY GUIDE TO FBI PROFILING AND GEOGRAPHICAL AND STATISTICAL PROFILING.

CLINICAL PSYCHOLOGY

FORMULATION IN PSYCHOTHERAPY

PERSONALITY PSYCHOLOGY AND INDIVIDUAL DIFFERENCES

CLINICAL PSYCHOLOGY REFLECTIONS VOLUME 1

CLINICAL PSYCHOLOGY REFLECTIONS VOLUME 2

OTHER SHORT STORIES BY CONNOR WHITELEY

Blade of The Emperor

Arbiter's Truth

The Bloodied Rose

Asmodia's Wrath

Heart of A Killer

Emissary of Blood

Computation of Battle

Old One's Wrath

Other books by Connor Whiteley:

The Fireheart Fantasy Series

Heart of Fire

Heart of Lies

More Coming Soon!

The Garro Series- Fantasy/Sci-fi

GARRO: GALAXY'S END

GARRO: RISE OF THE ORDER

GARRO: END TIMES

GARRO: SHORT STORIES

GARRO: COLLECTION

GARRO: HERESY

GARRO: FAITHLESS

GARRO: DESTROYER OF WORLDS

GARRO: COLLECTIONS BOOK 4-6

GARRO: MISTRESS OF BLOOD

GARRO: BEACON OF HOPE

GARRO: END OF DAYS

Winter Series- Fantasy Trilogy Books

WINTER'S COMING

WINTER'S HUNT

WINTER'S REVENGE

WINTER'S DISSENSION

Miscellaneous:

THE ANGEL OF RETURN

THE ANGEL OF FREEDOM

CLINICAL PSYCHOLOGY REFLECTIONS

Companion guides:

BIOLOGICAL PSYCHOLOGY 2ND EDITION WORKBOOK

COGNITIVE PSYCHOLOGY 2ND EDITION WORKBOOK

SOCIOCULTURAL PSYCHOLOGY 2ND EDITION WORKBOOK

ABNORMAL PSYCHOLOGY 2ND EDITION WORKBOOK

PSYCHOLOGY OF HUMAN RELATIONSHIPS 2ND EDITION WORKBOOK

HEALTH PSYCHOLOGY WORKBOOK

FORENSIC PSYCHOLOGY WORKBOOK

Audiobooks by Connor Whiteley:

BIOLOGICAL PSYCHOLOGY

COGNITIVE PSYCHOLOGY

SOCIOCULTURAL PSYCHOLOGY

ABNORMAL PSYCHOLOGY

PSYCHOLOGY OF HUMAN RELATIONSHIPS

HEALTH PSYCHOLOGY

DEVELOPMENTAL PSYCHOLOGY

RESEARCH IN PSYCHOLOGY

FORENSIC PSYCHOLOGY

GARRO: GALAXY'S END

GARRO: RISE OF THE ORDER

GARRO: SHORT STORIES

GARRO: END TIMES

GARRO: COLLECTION

GARRO: HERESY

GARRO: FAITHLESS

GARRO: DESTROYER OF WORLDS

GARRO: COLLECTION BOOKS 4-6

GARRO: COLLECTION BOOKS 1-6

Business books:

TIME MANAGEMENT: A GUIDE FOR STUDENTS AND WORKERS

LEADERSHIP: WHAT MAKES A GOOD LEADER? A GUIDE FOR STUDENTS AND WORKERS.

BUSINESS SKILLS: HOW TO SURVIVE THE BUSINESS WORLD? A GUIDE FOR STUDENTS, EMPLOYEES AND EMPLOYERS.

BUSINESS COLLECTION

GET YOUR FREE BOOK AT:
WWW.CONNORWHITELEY.NET

www.ingramcontent.com/pod-product-compliance
Lightning Source LLC
LaVergne TN
LVHW011846060526
838200LV00054B/4189